ONTARIO

CLB 2909
© 1992 Colour Library Books Ltd, Godalming, Surrey, England.
All rights reserved.
This edition published 1992 by Coombe Books.
Colour separations by Advance Laser Graphic Arts.
Printed and bound in Hong Kong.
ISBN 0-86283-935-1

ONTARIO

COOMBE BOOKS

Ut Incepit Fidelis Sic Permanet. If you asked a random sampling of Ontarians for their official motto – and its meaning – how many could tell you? Probably not too many: Latin is barely alive in the province's schools, and Ontarians are diffident flagwavers at the best of times. Patriotic braying and breastbeating are just not the Canadian way. Yet, history's record shows that Ontario began loyal. And the prosperous peace of the present-day province seems to indicate that loyal she definitely remains. Just what modern Ontario is loyal to, however, is a bit of a mystery. And thank goodness. Debating what makes Ontario tick provides undergraduates and would-be Ph.Ds with an ever-ready theme for their essays and dissertations, and is always worthy of a few columns in the newspapers on a slow day.

Budding PolySci majors usually lay the foundation for their treatises with a recap of the province's British-to-the-bootstraps past. All goes well as the obligatory cast of heroes and mediocrities – there aren't too many outright villians in Ontario's past – do their bit – or try to – for Mother England.

Things start to bog down when the lights come on again following the Allies' victory over Fascism in WWII. War's end and the decline of the British Empire bring new faces to Ontario – and Canada: immigrants from Middle and Eastern Europe, and more recently from Asia, Africa, the Indian sub-continent, the Caribbean and Central and South America, who have rapidly changed the demographic make-up of Canada's major English-speaking province. What does the Queen of England and all the monarchy stand for to a Hungarian? a Pole? a Turk or Chilean? Not too much.

Yet mutli-cultural Ontario does work. To be sure, there are strains: prejudices, both homegrown and imported, do surface from time to time to sour the good life most Ontarians enjoy. And in a province as large – approximately one million km² – as Ontario, economic disparity, especially in the north, continues to be of ongoing concern.

But old and new Ontarians appear firmly united by an unspoken idea of what their province stands for – peace, order, security and, above all, freedom. Freedom to live and work where you choose; freedom from political, religious and sexual oppression, persecution and discrimination; freedom from the soul-destroying shackles of poverty. As individuals, Ontarians claim these freedoms for themselves; as citizens of the province, they are committed to according these freedoms to each other. In the process, Ontarians have established the judicial, economic, and social safeguards to ensure the peace, order, and security in which these freedoms may flourish. It is to these sentiments, at once lofty and pragmatic, that today's Ontarians pledge their loyalty. Mind you, on a hot day in July, an Ontarian's overriding loyalty is to "the cottage" – that wilderness retreat by one of the province's countless rivers or lakes that is the apogee of the Ontario dream.

For the most part, nature has been good to Ontario – a fact generously attested to by all those sparkling lakes and rivers that abound in Cottage Country and cover one-fifth of the province. This natural beneficence has done much to shape the cast of today's Ontario – and not only in the area of recreational real estate!

The Ontario of historical record is relatively recent:

the French, who were the first Europeans to settle here, arrived in the seventeenth century. They found the land cold and inhospitable – a vast and gloomy primeval forest.

The Native inhabitants, on the other hand, viewed the forest wilderness quite differently. To the tribes of the Cree, Ojibway, Algonquin, Mohawk, Huron, Oneida, Onondaga, Cayuga, Tobacco and Seneca nations, the forest offered food and shelter. And while these nations were not always the best of friends, all had an abiding respect for the land and its riches, both of which they invested with deep spiritual significance.

As to the land itself, we know that about 20,000 years ago Ontario lay buried deep beneath a year-round coverage of ice and snow. Over the next 10,000 years these Pleistocene glaciers were to melt and reappear four times. The present geological configuration of Ontario is the product of these recurring Ice Ages.

In the north, the craggy Canadian Shield, with its myriad lakes and streams, and its rich mineral deposits, dominated. The more recently formed landscape in the south evolved when the last great glaciation melted, some 10,000 years ago. The retreating ice created the Great Lakes and the lowlands of the St. Lawrence River, which took shape about 6,000 years ago. In time, the once ice-covered lands supported vast tracts of virgin forest. North of the Shield are the sub-Arctic lowlands of Hudson and James bays – today, as ever, a largely unknown, thinly populated region.

Archaeologists believe that the first humans to come to this vast land were nomadic hunters from Asia who entered North America via a broad plain which once linked the two continents. Over the centuries, hunting and fishing were to remain the chief means of securing food for the native peoples of the north. In the south, the more moderate climate encouraged the development of agriculture.

When the French arrived in Canada, they were deeply disappointed to learn that their quest for a northwest passage to the riches of China and India had come to a dead end in this rocky land of silent snow and brooding forests.

Fortunately for the French, the new land offered a consolation prize. True, there were no silks or spices, but these chilly lands offered riches in another

unexpected form: here were fur-bearing animals in abundance. And as the French soon discovered, the colder the weather, the better the beaver pelt for monsieur's fashionable new hat.

Unfortunately for the native peoples of the region, the arrival of the Europeans was to mark the beginning of the end of their centuries-old way of life.

Early relations between the Native peoples and the French started on a promising enough note, however. In 1610, two years after he had founded the city of Québec, Samuel de Champlain sent young Etienne Brûlé – he was just 18 – west to scout out the lands in present-day Ontario and to establish contact with the native peoples. The intrepid Brûlé accomplished his mission, living with the native peoples, learning their languages and earning their trust.

Brûlé paved the way for Champlain, who travelled to Ontario in 1613. On a subsequent trip, Champlain threw his support – and his European weapons – behind the Huron Indians in one of their many skirmishes with their old enemy, the Iroquois. From then on, the battles lines were firmly drawn between the French-Huron alliance and the Iroquois and their British supporters to the south of Ontario, in what was to became the United States. At stake was control of the riches of the fur trade.

French colonial policy had another, less crass, side – the bringing of Roman Catholicism to the New World. Missionaries from the Society of Jesus travelled west from Québec and Montréal to try to win the Hurons to Christ. The tireless Jesuit fathers met with varying success. In 1639, Father Jean de Brébeuf established a permanent mission near present-day Montreal. Sainte-Marie-among-the-Hurons included a church with adjacent cemetery, a hospital, dormitory, and assorted workshops. Alas, both mission and missionaries were casualties of the Huron-Iroquois hostilities of the late 1640s. The Jesuits torched Ste. Marie to prevent it falling to the Iroquois. Brébeuf and his fellow missionaries were captured and tortured – thereby earning the martyrdom so desired by the religious of the day.

But Jesuit setbacks pale before the misfortunes of the Hurons. Not only had they backed the wrong side – the French were ultimately outnumbered by the well-entrenched British – they were decimated by European diseases. Chicken-pox, tuberculosis, diphtheria, scarlet fever, smallpox, measles, whooping cough and influenza were all unknown in the New World before the Europeans arrived. As a result, an outbreak of any of these diseases would quickly ravage entire Indian villages. Epidemics of one sort or another wiped out half of the Huron nation in the six short years between 1634 and 1640. At the time the Iroquois launched their last murderous raids on the Hurons in 1648-49, Huron numbers had dwindled to around 12,000; a tragic decline from the 1610 population of approximately 30,000.

The sorry fate of their Huron allies did not suppress French ardor for furs. As the areas closest to French settlement became depleted of fur-bearing animals, the French moved relentlessly north, west, and south into the hinterlands. Along the way they built a series of forts and trading posts, the former ostensibly to protect the latter. The forts were also meant to remind the British that they were not welcome in French territory.

Fort Frontenac, the first of these forts, was built in 1673 on the site of present-day Kingston. Ontario's capital, Toronto, now sprawls over the site of another early French fort, built circa 1720. Some thirty years later, business was so brisk that the French erected a sturdier fortification, Fort Rouillé at Toronto, on the site of the present-day Canadian National Exhibition.

But it was going to take more than a string of undermanned forts to keep the British at bay. In 1670, Charles II of England gave a group of "gentlemen adventurers" a charter guaranteeing them the right to trade in those areas to the north of New France that could be reached from Hudson Bay. Three hundred years later, the Hudson's Bay Company is still doing business, making it the province's oldest mercantile concern. Also still in great demand, though no longer as trade goods, are the distinctive, striped Hudson's Bay blankets. Only now this superwarm material is also made into coats as well as bedcoverings. (Incidentally, Hudson's Bay coats were among the hottest souvenir items at the 1988 Winter Olympic Games, which were held in Calgary, Alberta.)

Already threatened by the numerically superior British to the south, the French were not about to ignore this further British intrusion on their northern flank. As fast as the British built forts to protect their new interests, the French attacked and captured them. Naturally the British counterattacked. These repeated skirmishes continued until 1713 when, under the terms of the Treaty of Utrecht, the Hudson's Bay Company was declared legal possessor of all the northern forts.

To many Ontarians, this early period in the province's history is the most colourful. To be sure, the imperial powers did wrangle repeatedly for supremacy over the region, and an ultimate showdown was inevitable. But while Paris and London scrapped, in the wilderness that was New France – one day to be Ontario – the undisputed kings were the *coureurs du bois* and the *voyageurs*. For it was the skills and courage of these men that made the fur trade possible.

Coureurs du bois were independent fur traders who opted for a wild, adventuresome life in the hinterland, free from the constraints imposed by service in one of the officially sanctioned fur-trading companies. *Coureurs du bois* are the Davey Crocketts of Ontario's wilderness mythology. Brave, strong, resourceful and skilled in the ways of nature, they bent the knee to no man.

Voyageurs, who were equally wild and heroic, were employed by the fur-trading companies to handle the canoes that were the transportation link in the fur trade.

Given the vital role the canoe played in Ontario's beginnings, it's not surprising that canoeing is today a great summer pastime in Ontario. Indeed, every kids' camp worth its name offers instruction in canoe tipping and promises at least one backbreaking portage before the summer's end. But only the most serious modern wilderness adventurer can hope to gain an inkling of what life was really like for those bygone *voyageurs*.

In the spring, the *voyageurs* would set out for the interior, their *canots de maître* laden with trade goods. The *canot de maître*, which was thirteen metres long and two metres wide, could carry up to 4,000 kg of goods, and was crewed by eight or ten *voyageurs*. A smaller canoe, the *canot du nord*, was used to travel northern rivers and lakes, and for situations when speed was essential. Throughout the summer months, the voyageurs would paddle thousands of kilometres. When rapids and other obstacles blocked their way, they travelled overland. Anyone who has ever backpacked in Northern Ontario on a hot, humid July day – cursing the swarms of black flies and mosquitos that torment one every inch of the way – has a small idea of what the *voyageurs'* life was like. But few modern trekkers travel eighteen hours a day, hefting portions of a canoe and loads of eighty kilograms or more on their backs as did the *voyageurs* of old.

But Ontario was not destined to remain a French hunting preserve. To the south, British land speculators began to eye the vast, almost empty acres of New France. Official sanction for the British to launch an attack on the French came with the outbreak of hostilities in Europe between France and England.

In 1758 the British captured Fort Frontenac. The following year the French fort at Niagara also fell. This devastating piece of news caused the French to burn Fort Rouillé themselves to keep it from falling to the British. One calamity followed another; that same year, 1759, the British under General James Wolfe defeated the French forces of the Marquis de Montcalm on the Plains of Abraham, thereby capturing Québec City, the heart and soul of New France. Montréal surrendered in September 1760. Although the Seven Years' War between France and Britain did not end in Europe until 1763, the losses of all her forts and major centres spelled the end of French power in North America.

But the French presence remained even after the Treaty of Paris, concluded in 1763, saw New France pass officially to the British. In fact, for the next couple of decades things remained pretty much as they had been in pre-conquest days. It was to take the American Revolution to launch Canada – and Ontario – on the first steps to a cohesive identity.

As students of American history know, the republicanism of the Thirteen Colonies did not sit well with all of Geroge III's soon-to-be-former subjects. Preferring to remain under British rule, a number of the American colonials decided to travel north to the new British colony. As the Revolution intensified, still others had no option but to flee north to escape the ire of their Republican neighbours.

Once in Canada, these Loyalists, as the newcomers were known, joined forces with the British troops stationed in Canada, and harassed the 'disloyal' Republicans at every opportunity.

The signing of the Treaty of Versailles in 1783 marked the official end of the American Revolution. And the beginning of a full-scale exodus of Loyalists to Canada. The newcomers were rewarded for their loyalty to the Crown with sizable land grants and the basic equipment needed to clear their acres, build a home, and start farming. Even with these incentives, the Loyalists' lot was not an easy one. Starting a farm meant the backbreaking work of clearing the wilderness of centuries-old trees and thick underbrush. All the essentials for survival – be they food, clothing or shelter – the Loyalists had to secure for themselves.

Some hungry early years notwithstanding, the Loyalists were to prosper. And in periods of respite from the hard work that was ever their lot, they devoted much attention to the political institutions – or lack of them – in their new home. Representative government was what the Loyalists wanted. A not unreasonable demand considering they had just recently lost their homes and livelihoods in defence of this concept.

Britain acceded to the Loyalists' request, in a manner of speaking, with the passage of the Canada Act in 1791. The act divided the colony into Lower Canada (Québec) and Upper Canada (Ontario). The reasoning behind the division was simple: the approximately 90,000 Canadians outnumbered the Loyalists (about 10,000 strong at this point), thereby ensuring the former majoring status in any elected legislature. Dividing the two groups and according each separate government would prevent this problem. So went the theory. In practice, however, power in both provinces rested with Crown appointees and an appointed Executive Council, rather than with elected representatives.

This decidedly archaic form of British government was not what the Loyalists had in mind. Even less appealing was the official policy of granting vast tracts of land to the Anglican Church. (While mulling over the loss of one of her most promising children, Mother England had decided that the lack of an officially sponsored Anglican presence in the Thirteen Colonies had been a significant contributor to the Republican delinquency that had fostered the American Revolution.) One-seventh of all lands were set aside "for the Support and Maintenance of a Protestant Clergy". This move not only galled the good folk of Upper Canada, it provoked intense bitterness in staunchly Catholic Lower Canada as well.

There was, however, one sweetener to this bitter pill, at least as far as the Loyalists were concerned. The act ensured that all lands in Upper Canada were granted in "free and common soccage" – that is, freehold tenure. This English method of landholding was in direct contrast to the French seigneurial system still operating in Lower Canada. (Under the seigneurial system, the landholder had to pay rents to the Seigneur, who was the chief landholder).

Land and politics were practically synonymous in those early days. Land grants attracted large numbers of Americans to Upper Canada, Americans who were often to perceive this northern land of unlimited opportunity as a natural extension of the United States. (There certainly wasn't much doubt where their loyalties lay!)

A series of intellectual and administrative lightweights was appointed by Britain to guide Upper Canada during those formative years. The chief exception in this lacklustre bunch was the province's first lieutenant-governor, Lieutenant-Colonel John Graves Simcoe. Arriving in the province in 1792, the energetic Simcoe – "effervescent" is the word most often used by historians to describe him – perceived his mission to be two-fold: to establish superior government in Upper Canada, and to win the recalcitrant Americans back to the bosom of the Empire. In Simcoe's scheme of things, the success of his second aim hinged mainly on the rapid achievement of the first.

In the four years of his tenure, Simcoe embarked on an extensive roadbuilding program – Yonge Street, at 1,100 miles (approximately 1,700km) the longest road in the world (skeptics can check it out in the Guinness World Book of Records) was begun in Simcoe's day – and set the wheels of provincial and local government and the judiciary in motion. Ironically, although he loathed republicanism, it was Simcoe who encouraged American migration to Upper Canada: the province was sorely underpopulated, he reasoned, and there were no hordes of British immigrants clamoring to come to Upper Canada. (Hardly surprising as Imperial Britain was generally disinterested in goings-on in Upper Canada.)

Torontonians usually remember Simcoe as the man who designated their now-great city the capital of Upper Canada – although he did change the then-muddy little community's name to York. (Name changing was quite high on Simcoe's priorities. In his burning desire to make "Little England" ever more English, he rechristened towns, rivers and lakes whenever and wherever he could. Lac Aux Claies became – surprise, surprise – Lake Simcoe; the Chippewa River became the Welland; the Toronto River, the Humber, and so on.) Simcoe also holds an esteemed role in local sensibilities as the namesake of one of summer's glorious "floating" public holidays.

(Simcoe Day is always the first Monday in August, thereby ensuring a nice long weekend at the cottage or the beach.)

Unfortunately, one of Simcoe's finest accomplishments is probably the least-known. Simcoe had long been an opponent of slavery, a fact that did not sit well with some of Upper Canada's Loyalist gentry who had brought slaves with them from the former Thirteen Colonies. This opposition notwithstanding, in 1793 the legislature of Upper Canada passed "an Act to prevent the further introduction of slaves, and to limit the term of contracts for servitude within this province." Upper Canada's Anti-Slavery Act was the first such legislation passed in a British possession, and laid the foundation for Upper Canada's 19th century role as a haven for black refugees from the United States.

No mention of Lieutenant-Governor Simcoe is complete without a passing nod to the governor's lady, Elizabeth. Mrs. S. was also an effervescent soul and, more importantly, a perceptive observer of life and mores in the new land. Her well-executed sketches of Upper Canada and her colourful journal, which is still in print, provide an invaluable insight into the doings in Upper Canada from 1792 to 1796, when the Simcoes departed for a new posting in the West Indies.

The post-Simcoe years saw stirrings for electoral and land reform and growing unease concerning the bellicose Americans on the other side of Lake Ontario. Popular wisdom proclaimed that war with the United States would likely prove a disaster for Canada. Not only were Upper and Lower Canada still sparsely populated, the former had a large potential fifth-column (eighty percent of Ontarians were of American stock), while the latter was inhabited by French-speaking *Canadiens*, who could hardly be expected to remain loyal to their British conquerors. So ran British fears and American hopes when, on June 8, 1812, the United States declared war on Great Britain, and by extension, on Canada.

Canada has long been dubbed "the peaceable kingdom" a sobriquet that, by and large, its citizens are quite comfortable with. Apart from twentieth-century involvement in two world wars and various international peace-keeping initiatives, Canada's "war" record, after the initial French-English struggle, has been limited to occasional fish and lumber disputes on the west and east coasts. And while history's record reveals a few short-lived rebellions, no great civil war looms large in the national consciousness.

The exception to the rule is the War of 1812, the war in Canadian history, but more especially in Ontario's history, for the effects of the fighting were felt most keenly in this province. Before the war ended, and peace was made in faraway Ghent on Christmas Day, 1814, Ontario was to suffer invasion and considerable privation. In fact, even two years after the end of the war, travellers remarked on the devastation everywhere evident between Niagara and Detroit.

To this day, all combatants claim victory in the War, although it's probably a non-event to the British, for whom 1812 and Napoleon are synonymous. Ironically, British troops are claimed by a number of historians to have been the decisive factor in the repulse of the Americans.

What repulse? counter the Americans, who can justly claim a victory over the British navy on the Great Lakes. (Too bad American marine successes were outweighed by the bungling ineptitude of many of her military commanders.)

Ontarians, of course, know better. As every schoolchild knows, the War of 1812 was won by Ontario, thanks to the courage of the civilian militia, the heroics of General Sir Isaac Brock, who sacrificed his life in defence of the province at the Battle of Queenston Heights, and the bravery of ordinary citizens such as Mrs. Laura Secord. (As Mrs. Secord's likeness and name are the trademark of a popular chain of candy stores, she's remembered fondly every time the citizens eat a French mint or nut Bordeaux bar, regardless of whether or not she trekked miles with her cow to warn the British of an impending American attack.)

Often overlooked, but of equal importance to the ultimate outcome of the War, was the support afforded the militia and the British forces by the province's native people, who not only fought with the Canadians, but also won the American native people to the British cause.

In the end, the War did what all Simcoe's roads, proclamations and public good works could not – it welded the colony into a truly loyal British domain. Perhaps if the Americans had not invaded, Ontario might have quite naturally evolved into one of the States of the Union. But they did, and in the process gave rise to an anti-Americanism that shopping sprees in Buffalo, winter vacations in Florida, and unrestricted access to U.S. television notwithstanding, still lingers in today's Ontario.

It's not that Ontarians don't like their southern neighbours – on the contrary, Ontario is arguably the most American of Canadian provinces and is least imbred with the distinctive regionalism characteristic of, say, Newfoundland, or Alberta, or British Columbia. Internally, it's another matter. But more on intra-Ontario regionalism later. Ever the commercial pragmatists, Ontarians are more than willing to do business with Americans – too willing, say some Americans, who point to the aggressive inroads made by some Canadian companies (usually Ontario-based) into corporate America's bailiwick. It's just that alarm bells go off in the provincial psyche whenever Ontarians feel that their neighbours are getting just a little too close. The recent Free Trade treaty between Canada and the U.S. – the current hot debate issue – illustrates this point well.

Prime Minister Brian Mulroney and his Federal Progressive Conservatives tubthump across the country in support of Free Trade, arguing that Canadians need open access to the U.S. market if the national economy is to prosper. The provincial premiers acquiesce, tacitly if not wholeheartedly. A definite holdout is Ontario's premier, David Peterson.

Peterson's opposition to free trade has little to do with party politics. (Peterson's Liberals occupy most of the seats in the Ontario legislature, while Conservatives (Tories), for decades the undisputed rulers of the province, trail a dismal third behind the New Democratic Party, Canada's social democratic voice of conscience.)

No, it's just that many folks in Peterson's Ontario feel that free trade with the mighty U.S. will kill many Ontario manufacturing industries, in the process throwing thousands of Ontarians out of work.

Current estimates claim that at least one-third of all Ontario's manufacturing jobs could be lost once free trade is in place. This gloom-and-doom scenario is not without merit. Much of Ontario's manufacturing sector consists of branch plants, offshoots of U.S. parents forced to establish a presence here if they wished to market their goods in Canada. With the lowering of existing tariff barriers, these companies may just as well increase production in the U.S. – sure to be a popular move in a number of economically struggling regions south of the border – and close their Ontario offshoots. And who could blame them? As Premier Peterson himself admits, the taxes are higher in the True North, and "it's colder" here.

Let many in the Maritimes rub their hands at the prospect of wide-open trade with their fellow eastern-seaboards in the New England states – it's always made more sense for New Brunswick to trade with Maine than with distant Manitoba anyway.

For Ontarians, what's at stake is their pre-eminent position as Canada's most populous, richest province – their role as custodians of much of the nation's wealth, and the arbiters of Canadian style and culture. English Canada's that is. Québec Province is the undisputed repository of all things French in North America. Of course, the rest of English-speaking Canada would dismiss Ontario's claim to superiority of any kind, except perhaps to its quickness in siphoning off as much of the national wealth as it could decently get away with. But that's another story. Besides, Ontario-bashing is a national pastime, as the province's effronted citizens are never slow to point out. (Just as on the home front, the rest of Ontario sneers at privileged Toronto. And what do Torontonians vent their spleen on? Why, the Toronto Maple Leafs, often front-runners for the Worst-Team-in-the-National-Hockey-League Award.)

Whether free trade will revitalize the Leafs, annihilate Canadian publishing (mostly Toronto-based), wipe out auto-industry centres such as Windsor and Oshawa, or lower lettuce prices in the middle of winter, all remains to be seen. What is sure is that the debate is not particularly new.

In the decades following the War of 1812, Ontario came to economic maturity. The fur trade, long the main reason for the province's existence, was eclipsed by the lumber trade. Great fortunes were made from the vast forests of Ontario, as loggers felled trees furiously to fill the holds of the timber fleets that sailed east across the Atlantic to the timber-hungry markets of Britain and Europe.

On the return trip, these hulks brought a cargo desperately needed in the growing province. Immigrants – scores of men, women and children, the dispossessed of England, Scotland, and famine-ravaged Ireland – were crammed into the rat-infested holds of the timber ships for the ghastly voyage to a new life in British North America.

Not surprisingly, the newcomers brought disease – typhoid and cholera, in particular – with them. And chronicles of the day are full of sorry accounts of some of these destitute newcomers whose hope for a better tomorrow ended with death in some roadside ditch.

The survivors brought an unrelenting capacity for hard work – and, all too often, a hefty cargo of old-country prejudices. Protestant Orange and Catholic Green got on no better in the new land than they had in the old. Indeed, even now, the granting of full state financing for Catholic education up to the end of high school has provoked much outspoken criticism, and is said to have been one of the causes of the provincial Tories' recent fall from power after decades of rule.

The foundation of Ontario's two-tier school system – non-denominational public schools and so-called separate, that is, religious-based, schools – dates back to one of the better-known documents in Canadian history – the Durham Report.

Lord Durham, "Radical Jack" to his Whig friends in Westminster, was sent to Upper and Lower Canada in 1838 to investigate the causes of the uprisings that had taken place in both provinces the previous year. The rebellions, led by William Lyon Mackenzie in Upper Canada and by Louis-Joseph Papineau in Lower Canada, were primarily in support of that responsible, representative government which Loyalists had been clamoring for in Simcoe's day. (By the mid 1830s, government rested squarely in the hands of an oligarchy known are the Family Compact – an elite group who kept all power and patronage, be it military, judicial, or commercial – to themselves. Capital "L" Loyalists, the Family Compact did it all for England, at least so they claimed. Many were veterans of 1812, so no one doubted their antipathy towards any looser form of government that might smack of American republicanism.)

Although both rebellions had failed, the fact that they had happened at all was sufficient to make the Colonial Office sit up and take some notice of Britain's North American colony. Enter Lord Durham.

After touring the colony, Lord Durham retired to write his report. (In doing so, he undoubtedly set in motion a practice still very popular in Canada – and Ontario – the holding of much-heralded and usually very costly Royal Commissions of Inquiry, to be followed by the obligatory Royal Commission Report.) Like many a latter-day report, Durham's opus had results far different from his recommendations. Basically, Durham's report called for the protestantization of the *Canadiens* of Lower Canada. This "conversion" would be accomplished by merging the two provinces into one (an Anglican one) and the establishment of a non-denominational public school system.

Durham also urged Britain to grant responsible government. Colonial history being the usual mix of greed and benign stupidity that it is, the Crown said "yes" to union, and "no" to responsible government. The Act of Union, which joined Upper and Lower Canada, was passed in 1840. For the next twenty-five years, the province of Canada consisted of Canada East (Québec) and Canada West (Ontario). Not surprisingly, this move united the French in their resistance to all efforts at enforced Anglicization. Efforts at establishing a supposedly unifying non-denominational school system also had exactly the opposite results. In the end, however, long-denied responsible government was granted.

So long coming, responsible government, once enacted, soon proved inadequate. Immigration, the dawning railway age, the opening up of the lands west of Ontario, and the growth of the manufacturing sector placed ever greater and more complex demands on the political structure of the colony. Additional governmental reform was definitely needed.

The result, the British North America Act, passed July 1, 1867, created the Dominion of Canada. By the terms of confederation, the federal government took responsibility for national, international and key economic affairs, while the provincial governments retained jurisdiction over regional affairs, and that old political hot potato, education.

July 1st is definitely a Very Important Holiday for Canadians. For one thing, it's the beginning of summer vacation for the nation's youngsters. For everyone, it's a day for barbecues and picnics, civic-sponsored outdoor concerts, and massive firework displays and – dare we say it – the experience of feeling a little patriotic lump in the throat when the band strikes up *O Canada*.

For Ontario, July 1st marks the day when the province came officially by its name. On July 1, 1867, Canada West became the Province of Ontario. (The other July 1st birthday celebrants are Québec, Nova Scotia, and new Brunswick, Canada's other founding provinces.) The name "Ontario" is from an Indian word usually translated as "beautiful lake" or "beautiful water".

Back in 1867, Ontario's northern border went only as far as the Canadian Shield, the source of the rivers that run into Hudson Bay. The Hudson's Bay Company owned everything north of this point. Two years later, the federal government bought this vast holding from the Bay and, shortly thereafter, Ontario's official northern boundary was fixed at James and Hudson bays.

Many of Ontario's successes – and setbacks – stem from its unwieldy size. (The province is Canada's second largest; only Québec is bigger than Ontario.)

Although Ontarians are probably the least regionally minded of all Canadians, this condition should not be attributed to an excess of patriotic federalist spirit. On the contrary, it seems to stem from the excessive regionalism that has long existed within the province itself.

Nature, in the form of the Canadian Shield, created the most obvious division in the province. To the south of the Shield lies southern Ontario, the province's agricultural and industrial base.

Ontario contains the largest amount of Class I agricultural land in the country, and most of it is found south of the Shield. Hogs, dairy and beef cattle are all raised in southern Ontario, as are a wide range of cash and forage crops. Stone fruit orchards and vineyards predominate in the Niagara region. (No group opposes Free Trade more vehemently than the wine producers of Niagara, who fear that the new economic order will cause their developing enterprises to drown in a sea of inexpensive Californian imports.)

Like their counterparts in the rest of Canada - indeed in all of North America – Ontario farmers face an uphill battle to make a decent living from the land. Foreclosures have led to the formation of farmers' survival groups, who have not been slow to set their own case before the general public.

While the decline of Ontario as a primarily agricultural society began with the post-Confederation industrial boom, the values of small-town, rural Ontario still exert a powerful grip on the provincial persona. Although Ontario citizens enjoy a plethora of social benefits, there is a general feeling still abroad in the land that hard work and thrift bring their own rewards. Mainstream Americans would probably recognize the "no-free-lunch" attitude of many working Ontarians; what they might find harder to understand is the apparent willingness of these self-same Ontarians to ensure adequate safety nets for those citizens who can't provide all of life's necessitities for themselves.

Nineteenth-century industrial Ontario was a slave to the notion of progress at all costs. In a province as vast as Ontario, profitable industrialization called for transportation of the new goods from the growing communities of southern Ontario to markets in the hinterlands across the border. Not surprisingly, water transportation routes were extremely important. Politics as well as economics often spurred some of the canal-building activities that occupied Ontario's attention during the mid-nineteenth century. For example, the Welland Canal, the brainchild of William Hamilton Merritt, was Ontario's answer to the challenge posed by the American construction of the Erie Canal.

The St. Lawrence Seaway-Great Lakes Seaway is an example of one of those fortuitous instances where Ontario and her southern neighbours decided to work together for the common good. (Mind you, the U.S. was not all that keen on the Seaway at first: the U.S. Senate didn't get around to ratifying a 1941 treaty relating to the proposed seaway until 1949.) The Seaway links the five Great Lakes – Ontario, Erie, Superior, Huron and Michigan – and the St. Lawrence River with the Atlantic Ocean. A stupendous engineering and construction feat, the Seaway cost Canada a staggering $330 million and the U.S. $130 million. Canada has since paid a further $300 million to improve the Welland Canal, which is used by ships to circumvent the turbulent Niagara River. The Seaway was officially opened by Her Majesty Queen Elizabeth II, Prime Minister John Diefenbaker and President Dwight D. Eisenhower on June 26, 1959.

In time, railways replaced canals as the major means of transportation. "Railway fever" spread very rapidly. In 1850, for example Canada had 110km of railway track; ten years later it had 3,200km. As the old century gave way to the new, Ontario was dissected by a network of railway tracks. Control of these vital transport routes lay with a few major concerns – the Grand Trunk, the Canadian Northern, the Canadian Pacific and the Timiskaming and Northern Ontario. Corporate shakedowns have since reduced these numbers, while the growth of road and air transport

has curtailed railway supremacy not only in Ontario, but all across North America.

In their heyday, the railways cemented Ontario's position as the hub of Canada, for the railways opened up the western prairies to settlement. Ontario was only too happy to furnish the trains – and the supplies – needed to transport the newcomers and help them get started in their new homes.

The kingpin in all this bustling prosperity was Toronto – then as now the financial centre of the country. (Yes, it's true that only Vancouver and Montréal have officially been declared Canada's two International Banking Centres, and yes, Toronto did sulk and cry foul over the decision. But not for long. Such grand designations notwithstanding, the corporate and financial action in Canada takes place in the glittering towers of Toronto's Bay Street and everybody at home and abroad knows it.)

The railways also played a major role in opening up Ontario's north. Railway construction itself revealed the rich, untapped mineral deposits of the region. The vast nickel deposits responsible for bustling Sudbury's existence, for example, were unearthed during the building of the CPR. The Sudbury basin, which may have been formed millions of years ago by a gigantic meteoric impact, also contains gold, silver, cobalt and platinum.

What nickel is to Sudbury, gold is to Kirkland Lake – the town is actually built on gold-bearing rock – silver to Cobalt, copper to Copper Cliff, and uranium to Elliot Lake. Minerals brought prosperity and population to the north. Unfortunately, international mineral markets are notoriously fickle. As a result, Northern Ontario's fortunes are too often characterized by boom-bust cycles, with the downswings causing considerable hardships.

Industrial Ontario's development had one more imporant contributing factor – hydroelectric power. Although private companies initially leased the right to harness water power from the provincial government, which had jurisdiction over all inland water, the province ultimately attained control over the production and distribution of all hydroelectric power in Ontario. The mechanism for this control was, and still is, the Ontario Hydro Commission. Provincial control over hydro was designed to ensure all Ontario industries equal access to this vital power source. Sir Adam Beck, the undisputed father of Ontario Hydro, lives on in permanent, if somewhat noisy, memory at the giant generating stations at mighty Niagara Falls that bear his name.

But it would take more than railroads, or massive public utilities, or shared trials and tribulations such as the Great Depression and two world wars, to make a province as disparate as Ontario into an homogeneous entity. Mature Ontario, however, has learned to view its regional – and ethnographic – differences as strengths; contributors to the uniqueness and vitality of provincial life.

Incredible! is the favourite adjective used by the Ministry of Tourism to describe Ontario. The province offers visitors and locals alike a wealth of recreational opportunities – everything from white water rafting and wilderness backpacking in the summer, to icefishing, snowshoeing and skiing (cross-country and downhill) in the winter. Scattered throughout the province are snug little inns – usually faithfully restored pioneer structures, complete with antique furnishings, that offer not only superb accommodation, and a chance to sample Ontario country cooking at its best, but also a much-needed respite from the stress and strain of city living. Roads are excellent and scenic routes abound, so discovering Ontario's delights is no hardship. In fact, the biggest problem facing Ontarians and tourists is deciding just what to sample first.

The big city lights of Toronto are an undeniable attraction. In Toronto, you'll find all the glitz of New York (well, almost all), with a patina of British courtesy to deflect the hard edges, and a marvellous infusion of cosmopolitan j*oie de vivre* – thanks to all those newcomers from Asia, India, Europe, Central and South America, Africa and the Caribbean who have settled in Toronto in recent years.

In addition to being home to the aforementioned hapless hockey team, the Maple Leafs, Toronto is also a baseball town. The Blue Jays, Toronto's contribution to the American Baseball League, are definitely the favoured sons of the city. Trailing far behind the Jays are the Toronto Argonauts, TO's musclebound standardbearers in the Canadian Football League.

Clichéd though it may be, there really is something for everyone in Toronto. Hooked on history? Then the city's living museums shouldn't be missed. Toronto is a relatively young city, so seekers of cobble-stoned ambience may be a little disappointed. Two great fires levelled much of old Toronto and, more recently,

the wrecker's ball has taken care of a number of the survivors.

Fortunately, the city's love affair with the developer's crass view of what progressive Toronto should look like – all glass and steel and sharp edges – was very short-lived. And today many of the remaining old buildings have been restored and are now open to the public. Each comes complete with costumed staff, who cheerfully answer visitors' questions as they go about their nineteenth century business of making bread, or shoeing horses, or spinning, or cranking out a daily broadsheet, complete with the "latest" colonial news. Incidentally, the very modest price of admission to these museums entitles visitors to sample the baked goodies produced on the premises.

Science enthusiasts of all ages gravitate to the Ontario Science Centre, where hands-on participation is the order of the day. No kid can resist the chance of an instant punk hairdo which comes with taking part in the ongoing static electricity demonstrations. Other favourites at the Science Centre include a walk through the disorientation chamber, and hearing a whisper across a crowded room.

For stargazers, there are the astonomical and laser light shows projected daily on the great dome of the McLaughlin Planetarium.

Would-be space travellers will need a "visa" and "inoculations," courtesy of the Tour of the Universe, offered at the base of the CN Tower. This simulated space-shuttle trip to Jupiter, complete with processing through "Spaceport TO", circa 2019, certainly moves a lot more speedily than present-day flight arrangements in and out of Toronto's Lester B. Pearson International Airport!

Those born to shop should probably head straight for the Eaton Centre, a glassed-in complex that offers shoppers 300 stores, restaurants and services, plus 21 movie theatres. The Eaton Centre is named for Timothy Eaton, founder of the Eaton chain of department stores, whose flagship store is located in the Centre, naturally.

The Eaton Centre – and Eaton's traditional rival, Simpson's, located just across the street from the Centre – are part of Toronto's Underground City. The world's largest subterranean complex, the Underground City runs south from the elegant Atrium shopping office complex on Bay Street to Union Station, six blocks away. And yes, there are shops all along the way – in the Sheraton Centre, First Canadian Place, Toronto-Dominion Centre and the grand old Royal York Hotel. While the cash registers ring merrily below ground, multi-million-dollar deals are transacted above, for Toronto's extremely wealthy financial district sits squarely atop much of the Underground City.

Toronto's super-rich, and those with aspirations to join this by-no-means-small group, usually eschew the shops of both Centre and City in favour of the elegant boutiques and stores of Bloor Street and Yorkville. These days, as long as your credit card can stand it, there's absolutely no excuse for even the smallest Toronto babe not to be turned out in the latest fashions which Paris or Milan has to offer.

Not so long ago, dining out in TO was downright boring. Thankfully, rubber chicken and stewed beans now seldom grace the tables of the city's more than 4,000 restaurants. Whether your culinary tastes run to Thai, French, Chinese, Viennese, Malaysian, Polish, Greek, Creole, Ecuadorian, Ukrainian, Turkish, Russian, Japanese, Portuguese or Korean food, you'll find a restaurant in Toronto to satisfy you.

The list of Toronto's attractions could go on forever: theatre flourishes, the art scene is well represented (the Art Gallery of Ontario has the largest collection of Henry Moore sculptures anywhere), the Royal Ontario Museum's Chinese treasures are world famous, the renowned National Ballet of Canada makes it home here, the Metro Zoo is unquestionably one of the most comprehensive and enlightened zoos in the world ....

The city abounds in safe, clean parks, and public recreational facilities such as Harborfront, and the ongoing waterfront development, ensure that a wide variety of cultural and outdoor activities are readily available to all citizens.

The subway system really works, the streets are free of litter and safe to walk at all hours, and Toronto has none of the poverty-ravaged slum districts that blight so many North American cities. In short, Toronto is an eminently livable place. Much of the reason for this urban success story lies in Toronto's makeup. For just as Ontario is a series of regions that have learned to pull together for the general good, so Toronto is a series of neighbourhoods that function in a similar way. These neighbourhoods, be they the Annex,

High Park, Swansea, Cabbagetown, Tosedale, Parkdale or the Danforth, are characterized by strong citizen identity and active citizen participation in local affairs. Neighbourhood action groups are a vital part of Toronto municipal politics, and woe betide the politician at City Hall, or at Queen's Park (the local name for the Provincial Parliament Building which is situated in Queen's Park), for that matter, who thinks to steamroll over citizen concerns. On a national level, the biggest political game in Canada is enacted on Parliament Hill in Ottawa, Canada's capital. Situated in eastern Ontario, gracious Ottawa, a harmonious blend of French and English, is built on a bluff overlooking the river of the same name.

The antics at the House of Commons aside – visitors are welcome to watch the Honourable Members in action – Ottawa is a delight to explore. It's a city of parks – there are more parks here than in any other city in Canada - spectacular gardens, both public and private, and fine buildings. Visits to 24 Sussex Drive, the Prime Minister's residence, are, alas, by invitation only, but the Governor-General will let you take a "guided" tour through the extensive grounds of Rideau Hall, the official residence of the Queen's representative in Canada.

Diplomats and senior-level bureaucrats – and Ottawa has plenty of both – usually like the good life. And Ottawa certainly gives it to them. The National Arts Centre offers a full range of cultural venues – everything from jazz, puppet shows, and underground film, to Shakespeare and Beethoven symphonies. Dining and wining are superb here. Not surprisingly, Ottawa's museums and galleries – the National Museum of Natural Sciences and the Canadian Museum of Civilization, the National Museum of Science and Technology, the National Gallery of Canada, the National Library and Public Archives and the Canadian War Museum – are ever-inviting custodians of the historical, artistic, and scientific doings that are every Canadian's heritage.

There's theatre aplenty in Ottawa (with performances in both official languages), just as there is in Toronto, but neither city can match the theatrical extravaganzas offered annually at Stratford and at Niagara-on-the-Lake.

Situated in the southwest of the province, Stratford's annual Shakespearean Festival is a major world theatrical event; the dream of local Stratford boy Tom Patterson, who liked Shakespeare's plays so much he couldn't see why they couldn't be performed professionally in Stratford, Ontario. The Festival became reality under the direction of that late giant of the theatre, Sir Tyrone Guthrie. From its modest beginnings in 1953 – opening night earned Sir Alec Guinness a standing ovation for the lead in Richard III – the Festival now consists of three theatres, and has added a number of different performance forms to its core Shakespearean offering.

Niagara-on-the-Lake's Shaw Festival is also a major annual theatre happening. Not only is the theatre world-class (and more than the works of GBS are staged at Niagara these days), the setting itself is worthy of acclaim. Niagara-on-the-Lake, in an earlier manifestation Newark, the first capital of Upper Canada, is one of the best-preserved and loveliest 19th century towns in North America. Visitors planning a summer weekend of theatregoing and fine dining in Niagara should book early, lest they find themselves without tickets or a room at the inn – literally; most accommodation in town is in restored inns and in small, period hotels.

Summer's end in Ontario has its own traditions, three of which are closing the cottage for the winter, viewing the fall colours, and going to a fall fair. The first is a sure sign to the province's kids that a new school year is upon them. The second promises a spectacular visual treat as everywhere the leaves turn from green to fiery red and blazing gold, and the third harkens back to early Ontario's agricultural roots. Agricultural fall fairs have been held in Ontario for well over a century. They offer farmers - and thanks to the 4-H movement, potential farmers – the opportunity to show off their livestock and their produce, and have

a good time while they're about it. Farm women, ever the mainstay of any agricultural operation, also display their skills at baking, preserving, quilting and sewing. Fall fairs also mean midway rides and cotton candy and corn-on-the-cob and a surplus of homemade pumpkin pie – in short, a good time for all. Perhaps that's why they continue to attract city people.

Or perhaps its a visceral nostalgia that draws urban Ontarians to these old-time country fairs. A yearning for an age when one had something tangible to show for one's labours. As the service and public sectors grow, outstripping Ontario's manufacturing output even as manufacturing once overwhelmed agriculture, concrete opportunities for experiencing the satisfaction of a job well done are lessened.

Today, one-half of Ontario's population of over 8.5 million live in or around four major centres – Toronto, St. Catherines, Hamilton, and Oshawa. There is no back-to-the-land movement afoot in these centres – or in London, or Sudbury, or Peterborough. But the sense of Ontario as a land of well-tilled farms and secure small towns on one hand, and vast, free wilderness space on the other, is both comforting and energizing to Ontarians.

Naysayers may well argue that in light of the economic reality of Ontario today – with its often hardpressed agricultural sector and the precariousness of many of its resource-based northern communities – this Ontario is but a myth: a myth that belongs only on the brooding canvasses of the Group of Seven painters, or in the gentle humour of Stephen Leacock's fiction. A myth it well may be, but it's a view of Ontario to which her citizens seem ever willing to remain loyal.

Previous page: a statue in Nepean Park, Ottawa, commemorates French explorer Samuel de Champlain, the Father of Canada. Left: Ottawa's Parliament Buildings, situated on a bluff overlooking the Ottawa River. Overleaf: the Senate Chamber in the Parliament Buildings.

Royal Canadian Mounted Police (left), more commonly known as "Mounties," guard Parliament Hill. A ceremonial Changing of the Guard (below and facing page) is a major tourist draw during the summer. Overleaf: Parliament Hill, overlooking the Ottawa River.

The Rideau Canal (facing page), completed in 1832, links Kingston to
Ottawa, providing an alternative waterway to the St. Lawrence River.
Above: Chateau Laurier, one of Ottawa's most renowned hotels.
Overleaf: fast-moving night-time traffic on Wellington Street, Ottawa.

Ottawa (these pages) was not laid out according to a specific plan and consequently lacks some the grandeur of other capital cities. Perhaps this is the essence of its charm. In winter, when the Rideau Canal (facing page) freezes over, it becomes a popular place to go skating. Even businessmen, briefcases in hand, can be seen skating to work.

The province of Ontario, where ninety per cent of the land is covered by trees, is one of Canada's most beautiful. Larger than most nations in Europe, it boasts spectacular and varied scenery.

Above: the shaded floor of a forest on Hill Island. Right: richly-forested islands in the St. Lawrence. Overleaf: Thousand Islands/Ivy Lea Bridge, spanning Georgina and Constance Islands.

Kingston, one-time capital of the province of Canada, boasts buildings like City Hall (facing page) and exotic Bellevue House (below). Left: a military display by members of Fort Henry Guard at Old Fort Henry, Kingston.

Trenton on Lake Ontario is linked to Port Severn on Lake Huron by the Trent-Severn Canal System. Craft travelling from Lake Ontario pass through the canal's complicated system of locks, rising 598 feet at Lake Simcoe before descending once again to Lake Huron.

Opened in 1965, New City Hall (left) has become one of Toronto's best-known features. Its distinctive, curved form contrasts with the traditional architecture of nearby Old City Hall. Overleaf: the Canadian National (CN) Tower, tallest free-standing structure in the world, dominates the city skyline.

Toronto, now characterised by the glass, chrome and steel of its modern buildings (above), has changed greatly since the 1940s. The magnificent Canadian National (CN) Tower (facing page), perhaps the city's most famous building, dwarfs everything around it. Overleaf: the mirrored face of the Hydro Building, Toronto.

Ontario Place (facing page and below) is a waterfront amusement complex and marina. Cinesphere (facing page), the futuristic centrepiece of the complex, houses a six-storey film screen. Right: boats moored near picturesque Scarborough Bluffs. Overleaf: the Toronto skyline seen from Toronto Islands, on Lake Ontario.

Toronto, which has now overtaken Montréal as Canada's largest city,
is serviced by a sophisticated network of roads (facing page). Canada's
Wonderland (above), only thirty minutes from central Toronto, was the
first of Canada's theme parks. Overleaf: the modules of futuristic
Ontario Place, supported on concrete columns over Lake Ontario.

Casa Loma (facing page), only a short distance from downtown
Toronto, is a modern-day castle. The ninety-eight-room mansion, built
by industrialist Sir Henry Pellatt, is now owned by the City of Toronto.
Above: a statue of Sir John Macdonald, standing outside the Ontario
Legislative Building. Overleaf: the bright lights of downtown Toronto.

The scenic Blue Mountains (facing page and below), near Collingwood, are less than an hour's journey from Toronto. The area offers some of Ontario finest downhill skiing. Right: ice canoe racing across Toronto Harbour.

Niagara Falls (these pages) is the largest waterfall in the world by volume, with water flowing at a rate of 35,000 cubic litres per second. The *Maid of the Mist* (above) cuts through the spray at the base of the Horseshoe Falls, giving visitors a dramatic, close-up view.

Point Pelee National Park (these pages), sticking out into Lake Erie, is the southernmost point of mainland Canada. The peninsula, one of the few uncultivated areas in southern Ontario, is home to many rare plants and animals, and is a bird-watchers paradise. Overleaf: a board-walk makes Point Pelee's marshlands accessible to all.

Georgian Bay (these pages and overleaf) is separated from Lake Huron by the Bruce Peninsula and Manitoulin Island. Flowerpot Island (left and below), part of the Georgian Bay Islands National Park is perhaps one of the most well known of the islands. Facing page: Finger Island.

Nickel production (above) is one of northern Ontario's major industries. Manitoulin Island (facing page top), south of Espanola, is the largest freshwater island in the world. Like Thirty Thousand Islands (facing page bottom), in Lake Huron, Manitoulin is a vacationers' paradise. Overleaf: the St. Lawrence Seaway at Sault Ste. Marie.

Pukaskwa National Park (these pages), situated on the shores of Lake Superior, covers an area of 725 square miles. The park's wild, remote scenery offers a chance to get away from it all. Overleaf: Pic Island and Ogilvy Point, silhouetted against a magnificent evening sky.

Agawa Canyon (left and below), north of Sault Ste. Marie, is a must on any tourist itinerary. The canyon is at its most beautiful in late September, when it is ablaze with autumn colour. Facing page: a pulp mill in the city of Thunder Bay, situated on the shores of Lake Superior.

Right: the rapids of Rushing River, now part of a provincial park. Overleaf: a magical sunset at Milbay on Lake Superior. Following page: Lake of the Woods, on the Ontario-Manitoba-United States border.